Just Joking

NATIONAL GEOGRAPHIC KiDS

Joke Pack 1

Say this fast three times:

Dracula digs dreary, dark dungeons.

Q What happens when a ghost gets lost in the fog?

A He is mist.

Q What do you call two spiders that just got married?

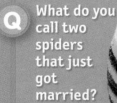

A Newlywebs.

Q What paces back and forth on the ocean floor?

A A nervous wreck.

3

Q Why did the
gum
cross the road?

A Because it was stuck on the chicken's foot.

Q How do you keep a turkey in suspense?

A I'll tell you later!

TONGUE TWISTER!

Say this fast three times:

Six smart sharks swam swiftly.

Q What did the
bee
sit on?

A Its bee-hind.

4

Double bubble gum bubbles double.

5

Bulldogs can weigh as much as 50 pounds—that's more than three bowling balls.

7

CUSTOMER:
Do you serve crabs?

WAITRESS:
Of course, sir. We serve anyone.

Q Did you just **pick** your nose?

A No. I've had it since I was born.

Q What has a big **mouth** and doesn't say a word?

A A river.

Q Why does it get hot after a baseball game?

A Because all the fans have left.

Where do smart **hot dogs** end up?

On the honor roll.

9

Bottlenose dolphins have little or no sense of smell.

KNOCK, KNOCK.

Who's there?
Kent.
Kent who?
Kent you tell who it is?

Q What did the chewing gum say to the shoe?

A I'm stuck on you.

Q What goes **zzub zzub?**

A A bee flying backward.

TONGUE TWISTER!

Say this fast three times:

Quick kiss, quicker kiss.

Q What is in an astronaut's favorite sandwich?

A Launch meat.

Q How do you catch a squirrel?

A Climb a tree and act like a nut!

Say this fast three times:

Felix finds fresh french fries finer.

Q Why did the **computer** go to the orthodontist?

A To improve its byte.

A parrot snake's fangs are located in the back of its mouth.

KNOCK,

KNOCK.

Who's there?
Hutch.
Hutch who?
You'd better take care of that cold!

13

Say this fast three times:

If a black bug bleeds black blood, what color blood does a blue bug bleed?

Q Why couldn't the teddy bear eat his dessert?

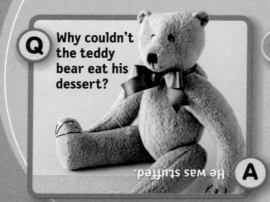

A He was stuffed.

Q What would you get if you crossed a judge with poison ivy?

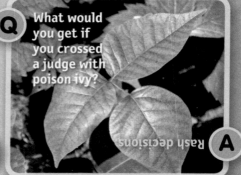

A Rash decisions

Q What did the beaver say to the log?

A "It's been nice gnawing you."

Q What is the worst thing you're likely to find in a school **cafeteria?**

A The food.

Sea otters use their stomachs as tables while they snack.

KNOCK, KNOCK.

Who's there?
Annie.
Annie who?
Annie body home?

16

Q Why did the **cat** put an **M** into the **freezer?**

A It turns into mice.

Say this fast three times:

Brenda's bunny baked buttered bread.

Q Why did the chicken cross the dusty road twice?

A Because she was a dirty double-crosser.

Q What do you call a nervous zucchini?

A An edgy veggie.

17

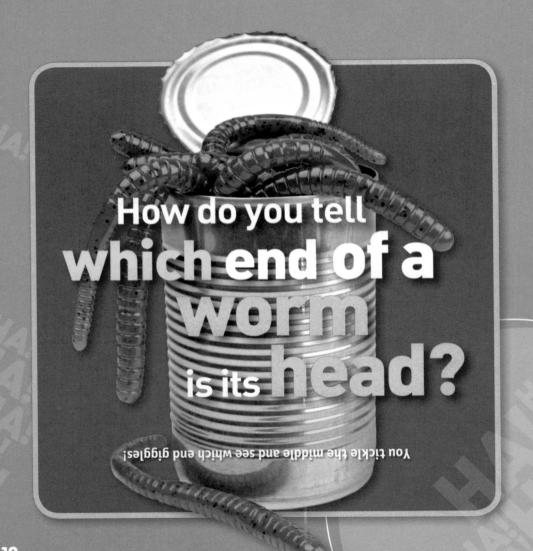

How do you tell **which end of a worm** is its **head?**

You tickle the middle and see which end giggles!

Q What do you call a computer superhero?

A A screen saver.

Q Why did the teacher wear sunglasses?

A Because her class was so bright.

Q Have you heard about the new **restaurant** on the **moon?**

A It's got great food but no atmosphere.

TONGUE TWISTER!

Say this fast three times:

Katie's kittens caught Kyle's kite.

Tigers have been known to eat up to 60 pounds (27 kg) of meat in one night.

KNOCK, KNOCK.

Who's there?
Alaska.
Alaska who?
Alaska only one more time to open the door.

Q Have you ever seen a line drive?

A No, but I've seen a ballpark.

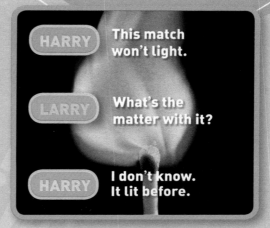

HARRY This match won't light.

LARRY What's the matter with it?

HARRY I don't know. It lit before.

21

Gentoo penguins are the fastest diving birds in the world.

HA! HA! HA! HA!

TONGUE TWISTER!

Say this fast three times:

Many an anemone sees an enemy anemone.

Q What travels around the world but never leaves its corner?

A A postage stamp.

Q What do you get when you cross a **turkey** with a **centipede?**

A Drumsticks for everyone.

Why are dolphins more clever than humans? **Q**

A Dolphins can train people to feed them fish.

23

KNOCK, KNOCK.

Who's there?
D1.
D1 who?
D1 who knocked!

To evade predators, a puffer fish balloons up by filling its stomach with huge amounts of water.